HAL•LEONARD®

KEYBOARD PLAY-ALONG

Soft ROCK

VOL. 2

T0081494

CONTENTS

ISBN-13: 978-1-4234-1789-7
ISBN-10: 1-4234-1789-5

Visit Hal Leonard Online at www.halleonard.com

HAL•LEONARD®
CORPORATION
7777 W. BLUEMOUND RD. P.O. BOX 13819
MILWAUKEE, WISCONSIN 53213

Don't Know Much

Words and Music by Barry Mann,
Cynthia Weil and Tom Snow

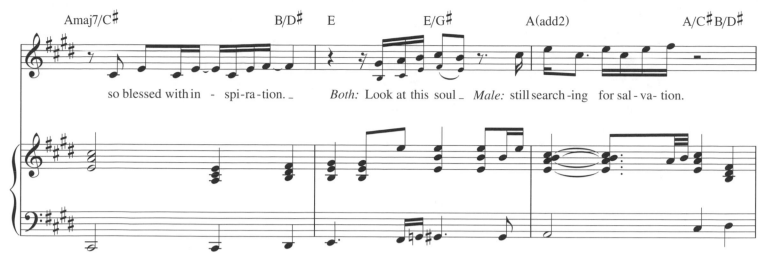

so blessed with in - spi-ra-tion. _ *Both:* Look at this soul _ *Male:* still search-ing for sal - va- tion.

Both: I don't know ____ much, but I know I love you, _____ and

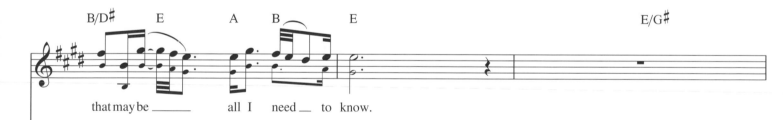

that may be _____ all I need __ to know.

Glory of Love
Theme from KARATE KID PART II

Words and Music by David Foster,
Peter Cetera and Diane Nini

We'll live for - ev - er
(We'll live for - ev -

know - ing to - geth - er ___ that ___ we ___ did it all ___ for the glo -
- er, know - ing to - geth - er.)

- ry of love. ___ *(1st time only)* Ooh. ___

We did ___ it all ___ for love. ___

Repeat and Fade

I Write the Songs

Words and Music by
Bruce Johnston

Moderate Ballad (♩ = 72)

I've been a-live

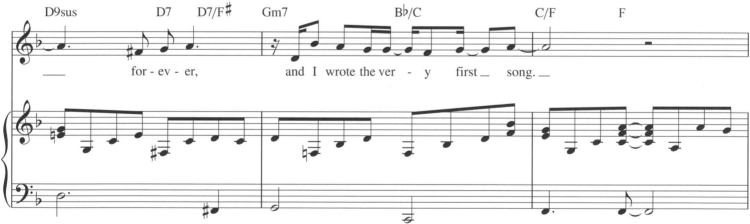

for-ev-er, and I wrote the ver-y first song.

I put the words and the mel-o-dies to-geth-er, I am mu-sic, and I write the songs.

14

and I've got my own __ place in your soul. __ Now when I look __ out __

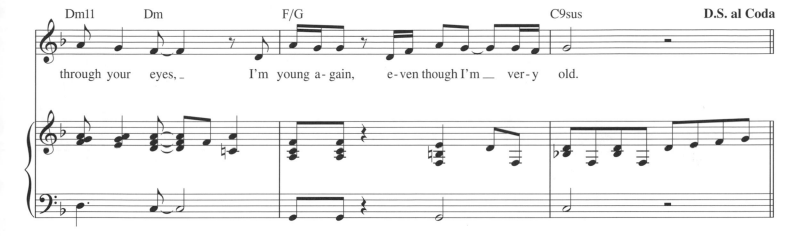

through your eyes, __ I'm young a-gain, e-ven though I'm __ ver-y old.

D.S. al Coda

CODA

__ Oh, my mu - sic makes you dance, and gives you

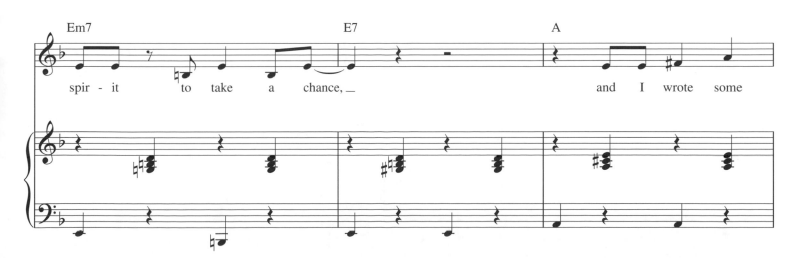

spir - it to take a chance, __ and I wrote some

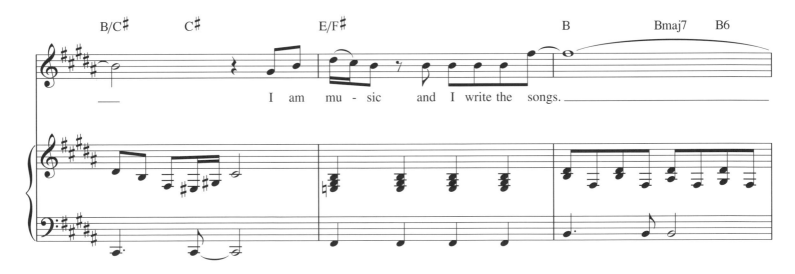

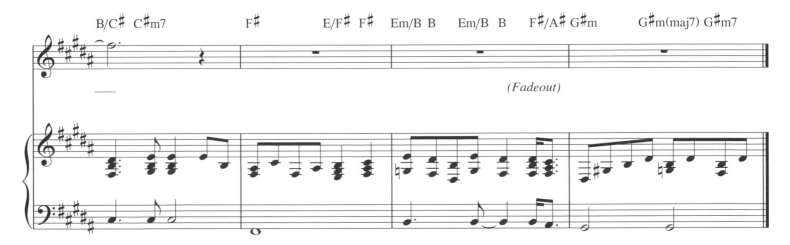

It's Too Late

Words and Music by Carole King and Toni Stern

And it's too ____ late, ba - by, now ____ it's too late, though we

real - ly did _____ try to make ___ it. Some-thing in - side _____ has died__

_____ and I ____ can't hide ____ and I just ____ can't ____ fake ____ it. Oh, ___ no, ___

___ no, _____ no, ___ no. _____

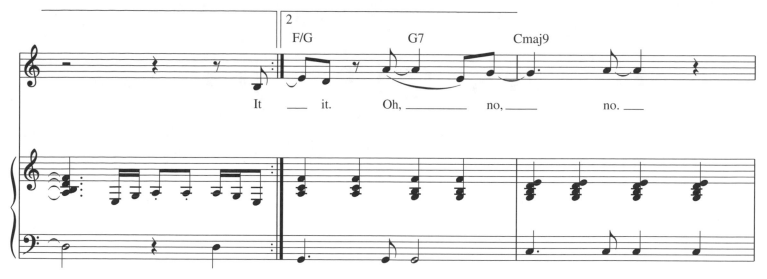

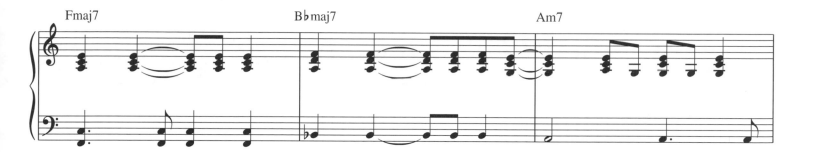

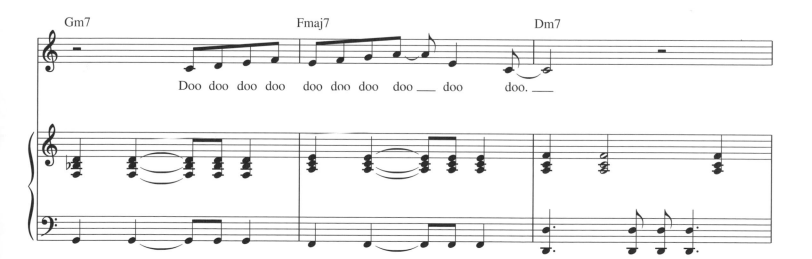

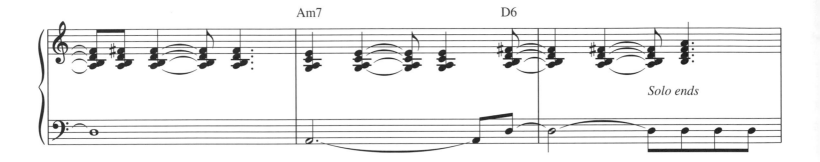

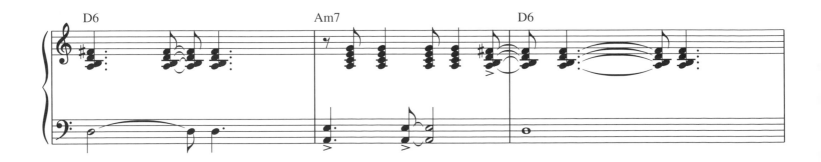

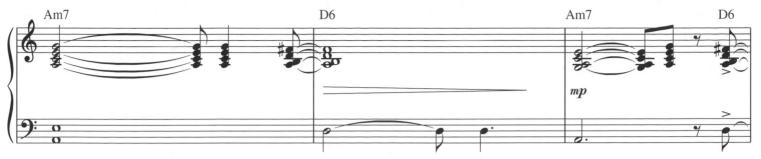

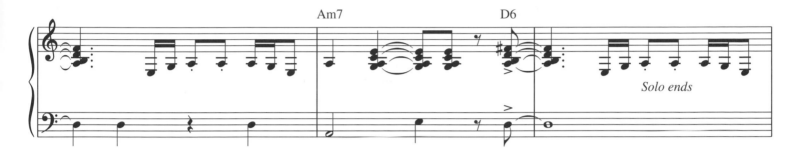

There'll be good times _ a - gain for me and _ you, _ but we just can't stay to-geth - er; don't _ you

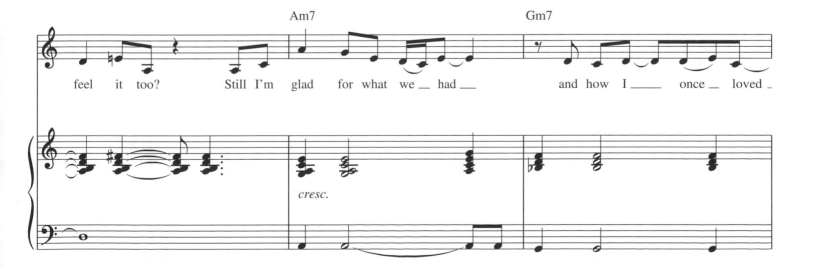

feel it too? Still I'm glad for what we _ had _ and how I _ once _ loved _

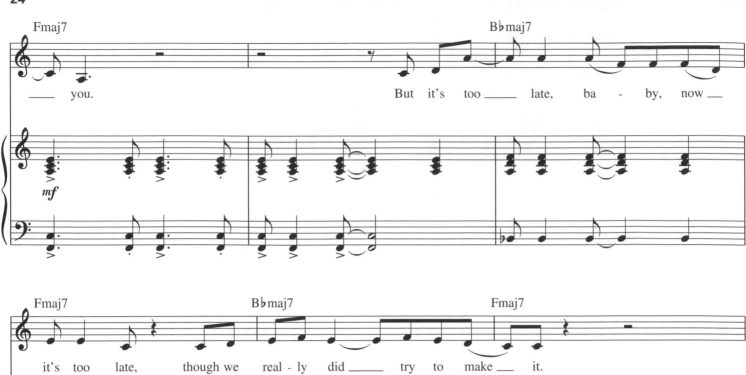

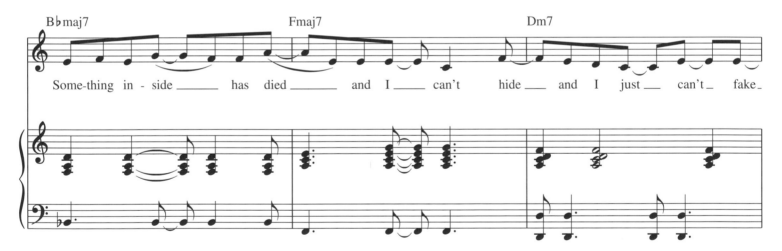

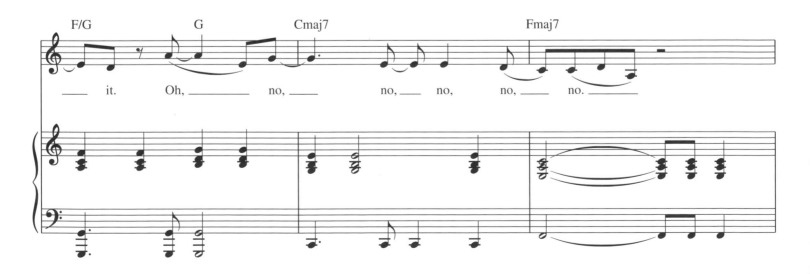

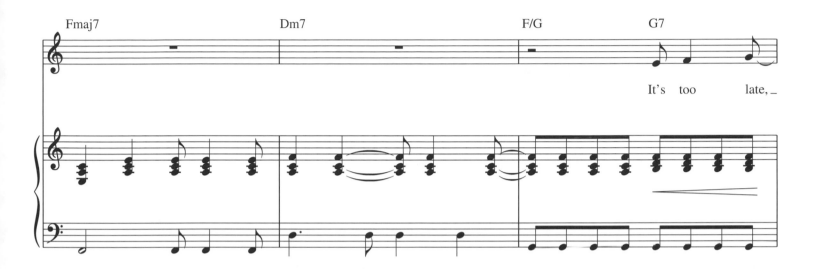

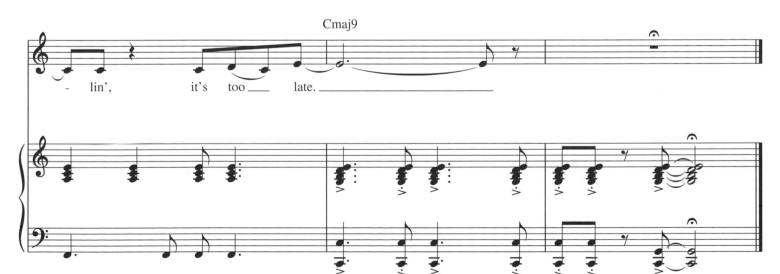

Just Once

Words by Cynthia Weil
Music by Barry Mann

back to be - ing stran - gers, won - d'ring if ___ we ought ___ to stay ___ or

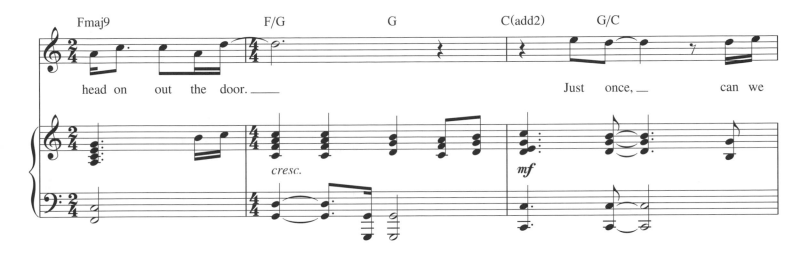

head on out the door. ___ Just once, ___ can we

fig - ure out ___ what we ___ keep do - ing wrong, ___

why we nev - er last ___ for ver - y long? ___ What are we do -

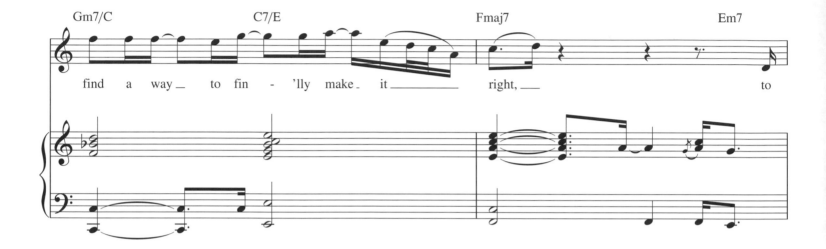

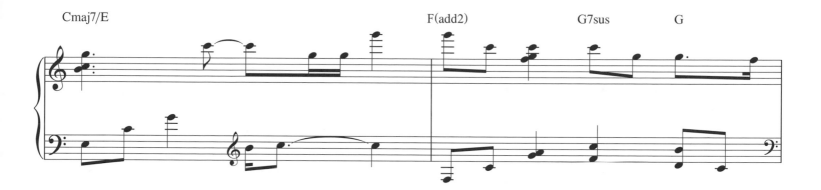

I gave my all, _____ but I think my all ___ may have been _ too much 'cause,

Lord knows, we're not get - ting an - y - where. _____

Where are we go - ing wrong?

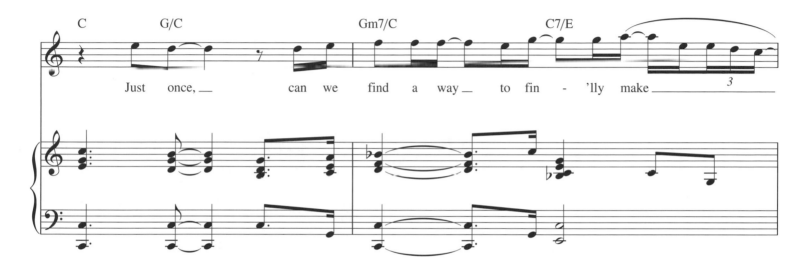

Just once, __ can we find a way __ to fin - 'lly make __

__ it right, to make the mag - ic last __ for more __ than

just one __ night? __ I know we could __ break through it if

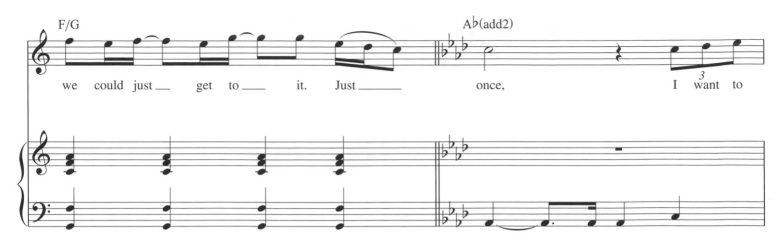

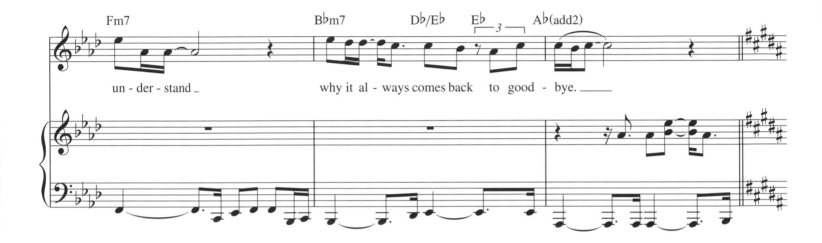

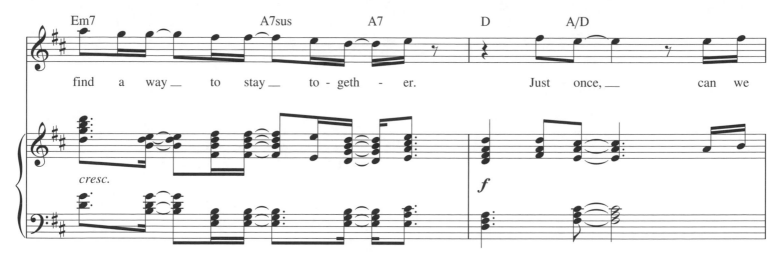

find a way___ to stay___ to - geth - er. Just once, ___ can we

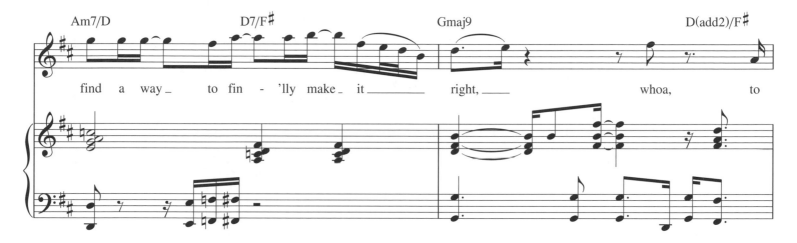

find a way___ to fin - 'lly make___ it _____ right, ____ whoa, to

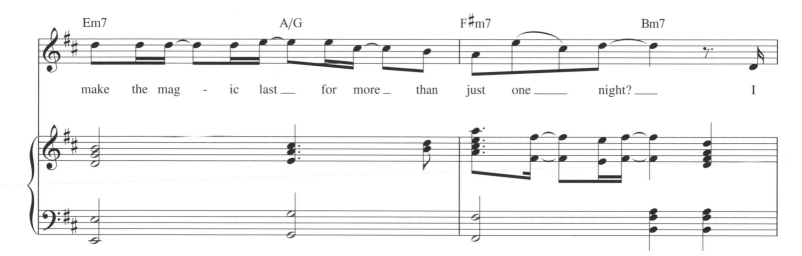

make the mag - ic last ___ for more ___ than just one _____ night? ____ I

know we could___ break through it if we could just___ get to ___ it just_____

D A/D   G/D   A/D

once.

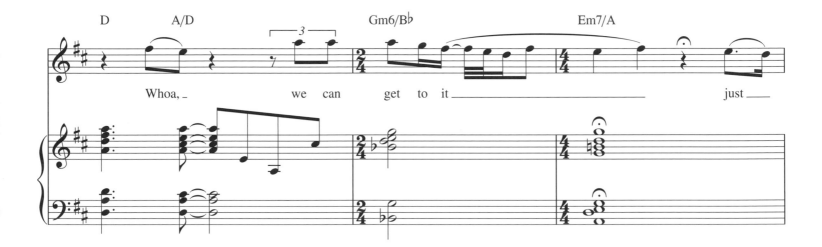

D A/D   Gm6/B♭   Em7/A

Whoa, _   we can   get   to it _____   just ___

D(add2)   G/D   Dmaj7/F♯

once. _____

mp

G(add2)   G/A   B(add2)

rit.

Making Love Out of Nothing at All

Words and Music by
Jim Steinman

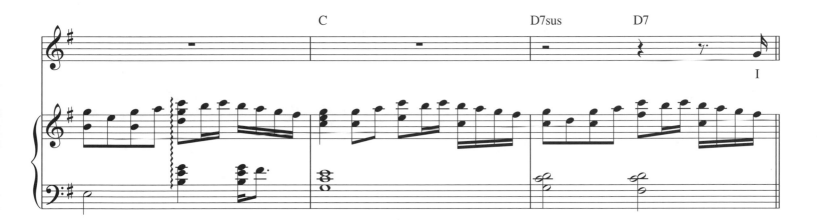

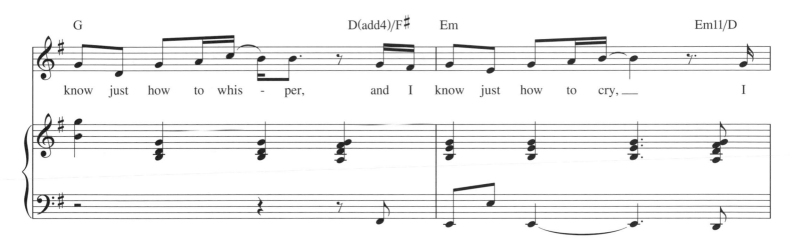

know just how to whis - per, and I know just how to cry, ___ I

know just where to find ___ the an - swers and I know ___ just how ___ to lie. ___ I

know just how to fake _____ it, and I know just how to scheme, _ I

know just when to face _ the truth, _ and then I know _ just when _ to dream. _ And I

know just where to touch _ you, and I know just what to prove, _ I

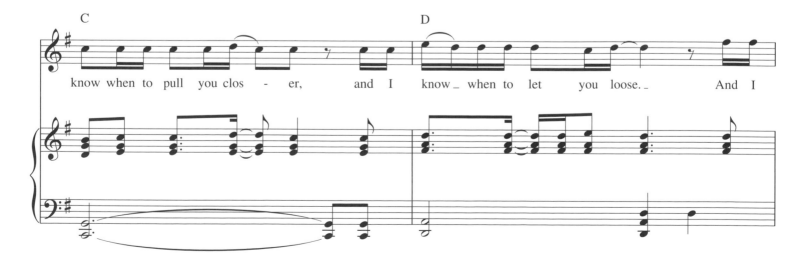

know when to pull you clos - er, and I know _ when to let you loose. _ And I

know_ the night_ is fad-ing, and I know_ the time's_ gon-na fly._ And I'm

nev-er gon-na tell you ev-'ry-thing I got-ta tell you, but I know I got-ta give it a try._ And I

know_ the roads_ to rich-es, and I know_ the ways_ to fame._ I

know all the rules, _ and then I know how to break _ 'em and I al-ways know the name of the game. _ But I

don't know how to leave _ you, and I'll nev - er let you fall. _____ And I

don't know how you do _____ it, mak - ing love _____ out of noth - ing at __

all, out of noth-ing at __ all, _____ out of noth-ing at __

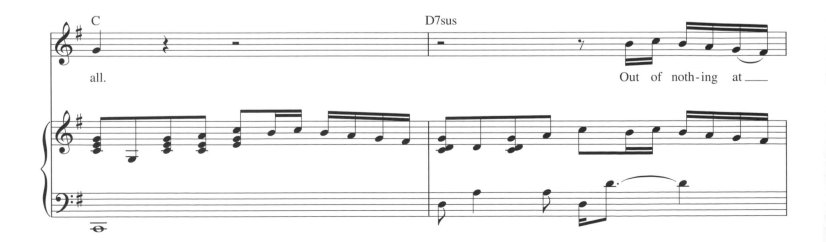

all. Out of noth-ing at ____

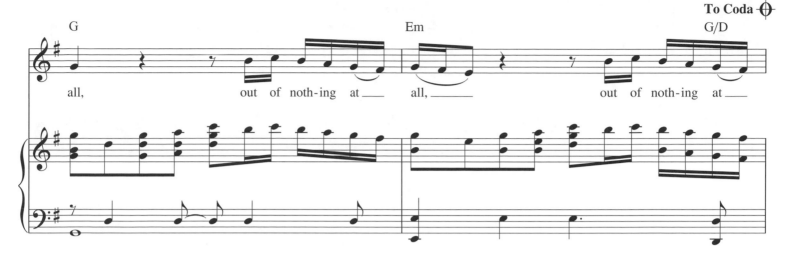

all, out of noth-ing at ___ all, ___ out of noth-ing at ___

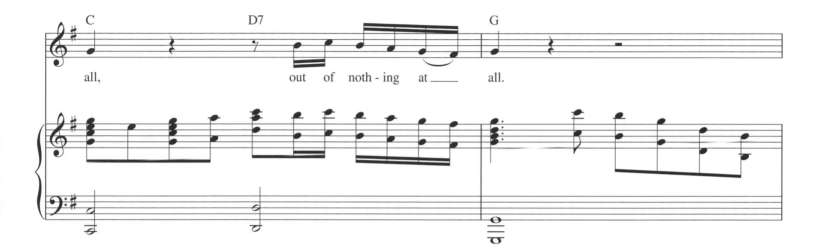

all, out of noth - ing at ___ all.

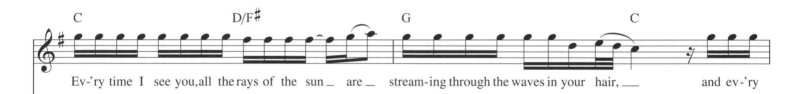

Ev-'ry time I see you, all the rays of the sun __ are __ stream-ing through the waves in your hair, ___ and ev-'ry

star in the sky __ is tak-ing aim at your eyes __ like a spot - light. __ The

I can make the run - ner stum - ble, I can

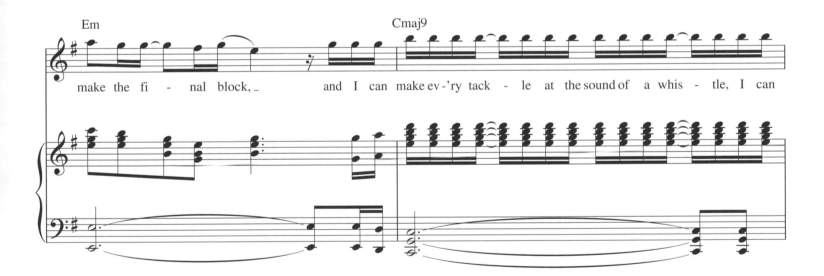

make the fi - nal block, _ and I can make ev -'ry tack - le at the sound of a whis - tle, I can

make all the stad - i - ums rock. _ I can make to - night _ for - ev - er, or I can

42

make it dis-ap-pear by the dawn, _ and I can make you ev-'ry prom-ise that has ev-er been made, _ and I can

make all your de - mons be gone, _ but I'm nev-er gon-na make it with-out _____ you. Do you

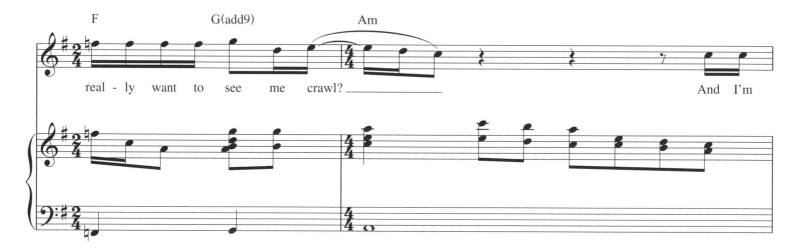

real - ly want to see me crawl? _____ And I'm

D.S. al Coda

nev - er gon-na make it like you _ do, mak-ing love _____ out of noth-ing at _____

CODA

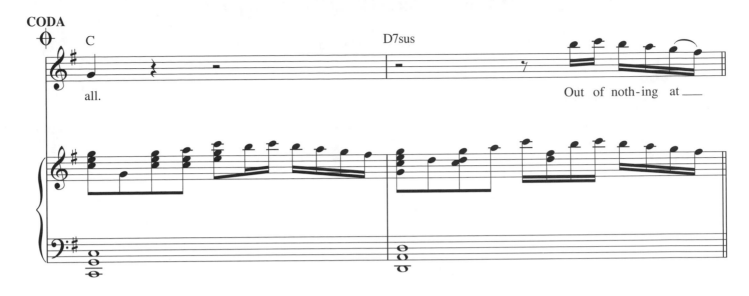

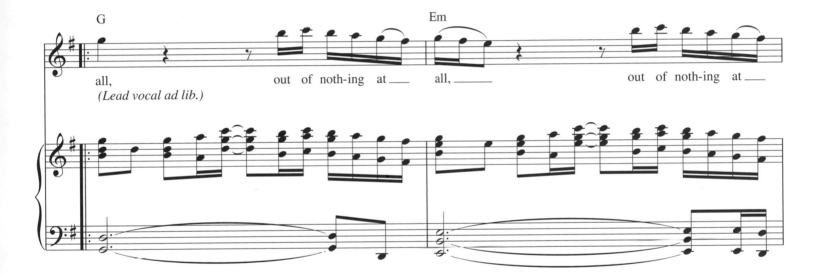

We've Only Just Begun

Words and Music by Roger Nichols
and Paul Williams

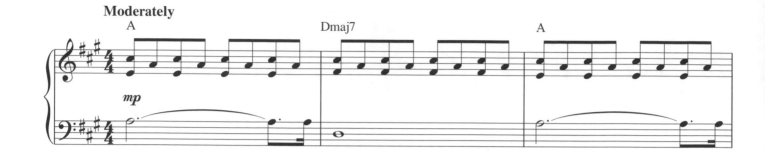

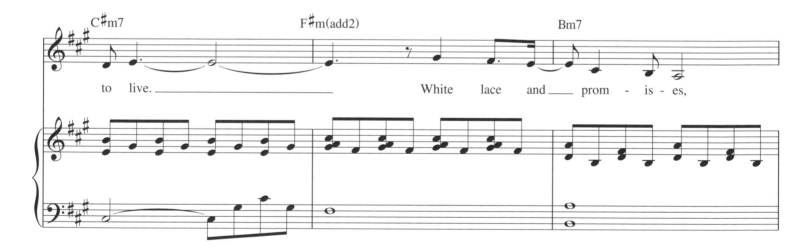

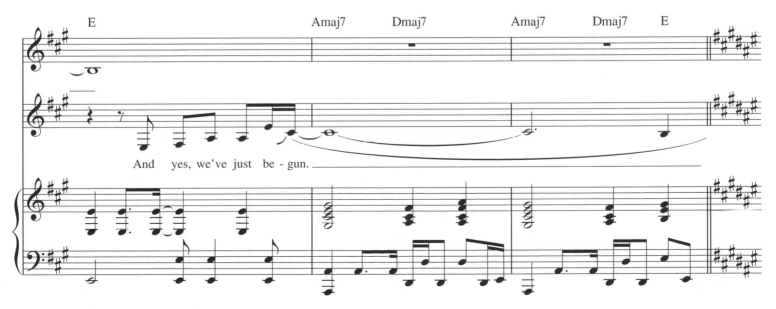

Shar-ing ho-ri - zons that are new to us, watch-ing the signs _ a-long _ the way, _

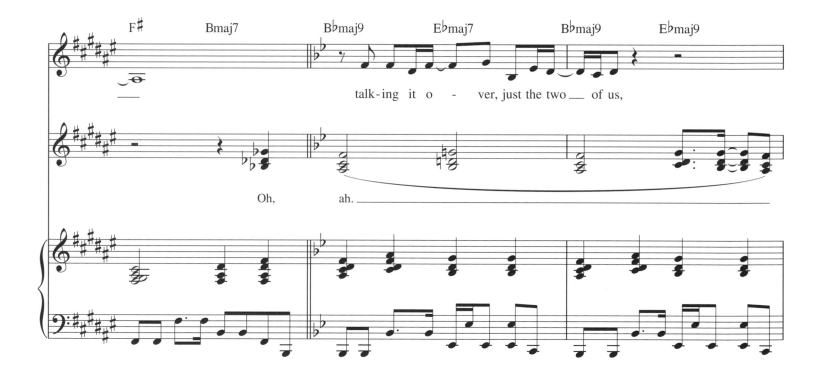

_ talk-ing it o - ver, just the two _ of us,

Oh, ah. _

work - ing to-geth - er, day _ to day, _ to - geth - er. _

work - ing to-geth - er, day _ to day, _ to - geth - er. _

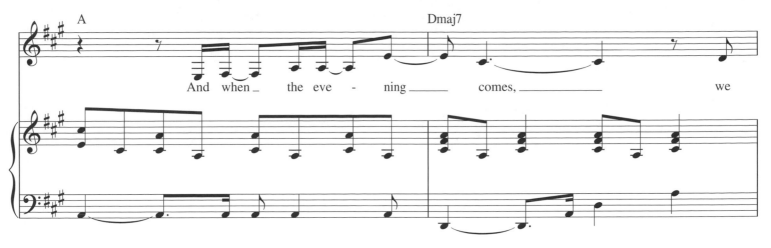

And when __ the eve - ning _____ comes, _____ we

smile. _____ So much __ of life a - head; __

Background: Smile. _____ So much __ of life a - head; __

we'll find a place __ where there's room to grow, _____

we'll find a place __ where there's room to grow, _____

we'll find a place _ where there's room to grow, _____

we'll find a place _ where there's room to grow, _____

_____ and yes, we've just be - gun. _____

Freely

You Are the Sunshine of My Life

Words and Music by
Stevie Wonder

- ways be __ a - round. _____

Female: You are the ap - ple of my eye. ___

For - ev - er you'll __ stay in __ my heart. __

To Coda ⊕

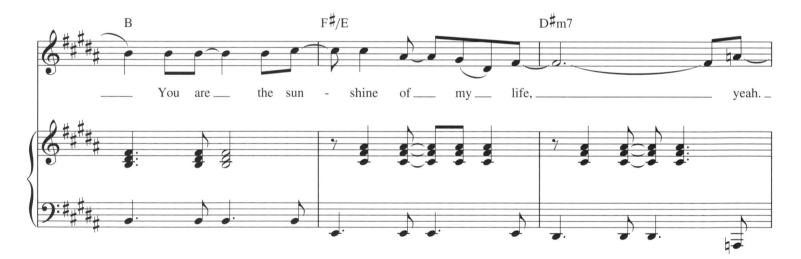

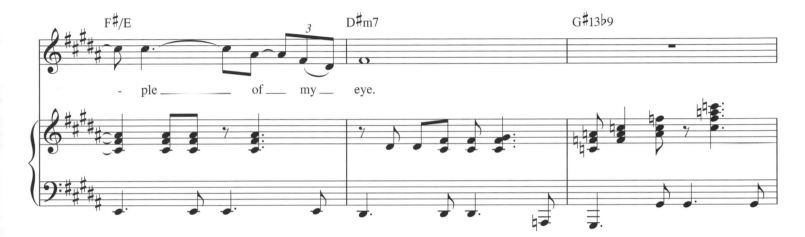

You are __ the __ sun - shine __ of __ my _ life, _____ yeah. _____

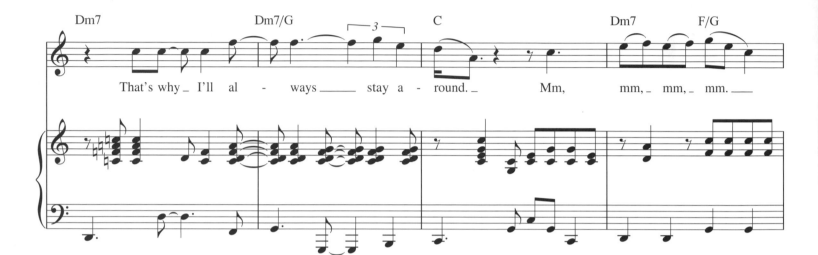

That's why _ I'll al - ways _____ stay a - round. ___ Mm, ____ mm, _ mm, _ mm. ____

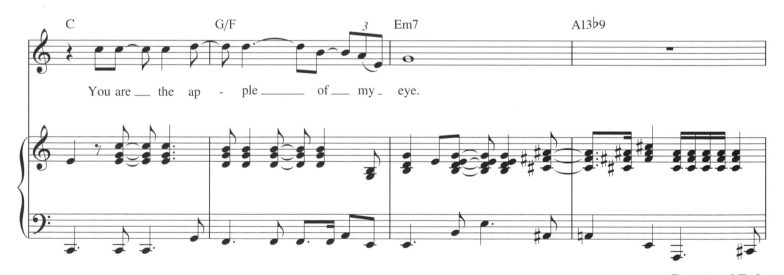

You are __ the ap - ple _____ of __ my _ eye.

Repeat and Fade

For-ev - er you ___ stay _ in the heart, _____ yeah. _____